Dogs Ca Kick

by Aiden Mark
illustrated by Monika Maddock

Harcourt
SCHOOL PUBLISHERS

Requests for permission to make copies of any part of the work should be addressed to School Permissions and Copyrights, Harcourt, Inc., 6277 Sea Harbor Drive, Orlando, Florida 32887–6777. Fax: 407-345-2418.

HARCOURT and the Harcourt Logo are trademarks of Harcourt, Inc., registered in the United States of America and/or other jurisdictions.

Printed in the United States of America

ISBN 10: 0-15-350345-9
ISBN 13: 978-0-15-350345-0

Ordering Options
ISBN 10: 0-15-350331-9 (Grade 1 Below-Level Collection)
ISBN 13: 978-0-15-350331-3 (Grade 1 Below-Level Collection)
ISBN 10: 0-15-357397-X (package of 5)
ISBN 13: 978-0-15-357397-2 (package of 5)

2 3 4 5 6 7 8 9 10   179   15 14 13 12 11 10 09 08 07

Dogs can't kick.

Many dogs lick.

Some dogs grow big.

Some dogs just dig.

Does this dog like food?
Yes, it looks good!

Dogs like to live
with you.

They can be good
fun, too!